Psalm 91:11

For he will order his angels to protect you wherever you go.

(New Living Translation)

Journey Prayer

Alone with none but thee, my God,
I journey on my way.
What need I fear when thou art near,
Oh king of night and day?
More safe am I within thy hand
Than if a host did round me stand.

Saint Columba (521–597)

Isaiah 41:10

Do not be afraid – I am with you!
I am your God – let nothing terrify you!
I will make you strong and help you;
I will protect you and save you.

(Good News Translation)

Photo: Chris North, Saint Columba's Shrine, Iona

Bless to me, O God,
The earth beneath my foot;
Bless to me, O God,
The path whereon I go;
Bless to me, O God,
The thing of my desire;
Thou evermore of evermore,
Bless Thou to me my rest.

Bless to me the thing
Whereon is set my mind,
Bless to me the thing
Whereon is set my love;
Bless to me the thing
Whereon is set my hope;
O Thou King of Kings,
Bless Thou to me mine eye!

From Celtic oral tradition – The Carmina Gadelica

Psalm 33:22

Let your unfailing love
surround us, LORD,
for our hope is in you alone.

(New Living Translation)

A Celtic Blessing

God to enfold you,
God to surround you,
God in your speaking,
God in your thinking.

God in your sleeping,
God in your waking,
God in your watching,
God in your hoping.

God in your life,
God in your lips,
God in your soul,
God in your heart.

God in your sufficing,
God in your slumber,
God in your ever-living soul,
God in your eternity.

Adapted from **The Carmina Gadelica**
– an anthology of Scottish poems, blessings and more,
from the Celtic Oral tradition
collected by Alexander Carmichael (1832–1912)

The Prayer for Protection

The light of God surrounds me,
The love of God enfolds me,
The power of God protects me,
The presence of God watches over me.
Wherever I am, God is.

James Dillet Freeman
Unity Worldwide Ministries

The Prayer for Protection follows a Celtic pattern. It was written in 1941 to bring comfort to those caught up in World War II, and later carried to the moon on Apollo 11 by Colonel Edwin 'Buzz' Aldrin.

Psalm 27:1

You, LORD, are the light that keeps me safe.
I am not afraid of anyone.
You protect me, and I have no fears.

(Contemporary English Version)

Photo: Susan Tilley, Lindisfarne

God be with you

May God be with you today,
to surround you on all sides with his love.

May Jesus be with you today,
to accompany you wherever you go.

May the Spirit be with you today,
to fill you with love, joy and hope for the future.

May Father, Son and Spirit be with you
today, tomorrow and always.

Anon

Matthew 28:20
Behold, I am with you always,
even to the end of the age.

(World English Bible)

Traditional Celtic Blessing

May there always be work for your hands to do.
May your purse always hold a coin or two.
May the sun always shine upon your window pane.
May a rainbow be certain to follow each rain.
May the hand of a friend always be near to you and
May God fill your heart with gladness to cheer you.

Old Gaelic Blessing

May the raindrops fall lightly on your brow,
May the soft winds freshen your spirit,
May the sunshine brighten your heart,
May the burdens of the day rest lightly upon you.
And may God enfold you in the mantle of His love.

Bless this day

all that I might see,
all that I might hear,
all that I might smell,
all that I might say.

Bless this day

all that I might comfort,
all that I might help,
all that I might guide.
Bless this day.

John Birch
Methodist local preacher and author
www.faithandworship.com

Photo: Ian Strachan, Lake District

Saint Patrick's Breastplate

May the Strength of God pilot us.
May the Power of God preserve us.
May the Wisdom of God instruct us.
May the Hand of God protect us.
May the Word of God direct us.
May the Shield of God
defend us.

Photo: Judith Merrell, Castle Rising

May the Host of God guard us.
Against the snares of the evil ones.
Against temptations of the world.
May Christ be with us!
May Christ be before us!
May Christ be in us!
Christ be over all!
May thy salvation, Lord,
Always be ours,
This day, O Lord,
and evermore.
Amen

Saint Patrick (387–493) was born in Roman Britain. At the age of 16, Patrick was captured by Irish raiders and deported to Ireland where he was enslaved as a herdsman. During his six years as a slave his faith deepened, he eventually escaped and returned to his family. Later, he was ordained a Bishop and returned to Ireland.

Saint Patrick's Prayer

Christ be with me, Christ within me,
Christ behind me, Christ before me,
Christ beside me, Christ to win me,
Christ to comfort and restore me.
Christ beneath me, Christ above me,
Christ in quiet, Christ in danger,
Christ in hearts of all that love me,
Christ in mouth of friend and stranger.

Taken from Saint Patrick's Breastplate, 5th century

Photo: Christine Wylie, Keswick

Psalm 3:3

But you, O LORD, are always my shield from danger;
you give me victory and restore my courage.

(Good News Translation)

Morning Blessing

May your day be filled with blessings
Like the sun that lights the sky,
And may you always have the courage
To spread your wings and fly!

Isaiah 40:31

But those who hope in the LORD
will renew their strength.
They will soar on wings like eagles;
they will run and not grow weary,
they will walk and not be faint.

(New International Version)

Gaelic Blessing

Deep peace of the running waves to you,
Deep peace of the flowing air to you,
Deep peace of the smiling stars to you,
Deep peace of the quiet earth to you,
Deep peace of the watching shepherds to you,
Deep peace of Christ, the Son of Peace to you.

Psalm 29:11

The Lord will give strength unto his people;
the Lord will bless his people with peace.

(King James Version)

Saint Brigid's Prayer

I arise today
Through a mighty strength:
God's power to guide me,
God's might to uphold me,
God's eyes to watch over me;
God's ear to hear me,
God's word to give me speech,
God's hand to guard me,
God's way to lie before me,
God's shield to shelter me,
God's host to secure me.

Brigid of Gael (c. 451–525)

Christian nun, abbess, and founder of several monasteries including Kildare, Ireland. Brigid is said to have had a healing ministry. Her mother was a slave who came to faith through Saint Patrick's teaching of the gospel.

Photo: Brian Cartwright, Making a Splash

Photo: Jonathan Leach, Honey Bees

God, my God

God, my Father, protect me.

God, my Mother, nurture me.

God, my Brother, work with me.

God, my Sister, comfort me.

God, my Friend, be close to me.

God, my King, direct me.

God, my God, find room for me.

Celtic inspired prayer
Author Unknown

A Family Blessing

Lord, we ask you to bless this family...
With a warm place by the fire
when the world is cold,
A light in the window when the way is dark,
A welcoming smile when the road is long,
A haven of love when the day is done.
For the blessing of this home we give thanks.

•

Our home is just a little house
But God knows where we live.

Anon

Photo: Judith Merrell, Country Kitchen

ARUN

You are the peace of all things calm,
You are the place to hide from harm.
You are the light that shines in dark,
You are the heart's eternal spark.
You are the door that's open wide,
You are the guest who waits inside.
You are the stranger at the door,
You are the calling of the poor.
You are my Lord and with me still,
You are my love, keep me from ill.
You are the light, the truth, the way,
You are my Saviour this very day.

From Celtic oral tradition, First century

Photo: Richard Ward, Bridge at Arundel

Saint Brendan's Prayer

Help me to journey beyond the familiar
and into the unknown.
Give me the faith to leave old ways
and break fresh ground with You.
Christ of the mysteries,
I trust You to be stronger than each storm within me.
I will trust in the darkness
and know that my times, even now, are in Your hand.
Tune my spirit to the music of heaven,
and somehow, make my obedience count for You.

Saint Brendan the Navigator (c. 484–577)

Irish monk, born in Tralee, County Kerry.
Sailor, shipbuilder, explorer and one of the Twelve Apostles of Ireland.
Adopted by sailors, travellers and the US Navy.

Circle or Caim Prayers date back to Saint Patrick and his followers when they would pray that God would encircle them with his love and blessings. Sometimes people draw a circle in the air as they say the words.

Circle Prayer

Circle me Father God,
Keep love within and hatred without,
Keep hope within and despair without,
Keep peace within and anxiety without.

Circle me Father God,
Keep strength within and weakness without,
Keep faith within and doubt without,
Keep light within and darkness without.

Circle me, Father God,
Surround me with your love,
Surround me with your protection,
Surround me with your peace.
Amen

Anon

Photo: Judith Merrell, Celtic Cross, Warkworth

A Blessing for the Home

God bless the corners of this house,
And be the lintel blest,
And bless the hearth and
bless the board,
And bless each place of rest.
And bless each door that opens wide
To stranger as to kin,
And bless each crystal window pane
That lets the starlight in.
And bless the rooftree overhead
And every sturdy wall,
The peace of man, the peace of God,
The peace of love on all.

Traditional Irish

Photo: Judith Merrell, Yorkshire

Irish Blessing

May your home always be too
small to hold all of your friends.

Photo: Jonathan Leach. Autumn Sunshine

Irish Blessing

When the first light of sun – Bless you.
When the long day is done – Bless you.
In your smiles and your tears – Bless you.
Through each day of your years – Bless you.

Psalm 113:3

From the rising of the sun to the place where it sets,
the name of the Lord is to be praised.

(New International Version)

Light and Peace

I pray that Jesus
The light of the world
Will bless you with
The light of life
The light of love
The light of wisdom
The light of wonder
The light of joy
Light without and light within.

•

May God bless you with peace,
Peace in your heart and peace in your home,
Peace for yourself and peace for your loved ones,
Peace for today's decisions, peace for tomorrow's plans,
May God's restoring, reassuring peace
surround you always.

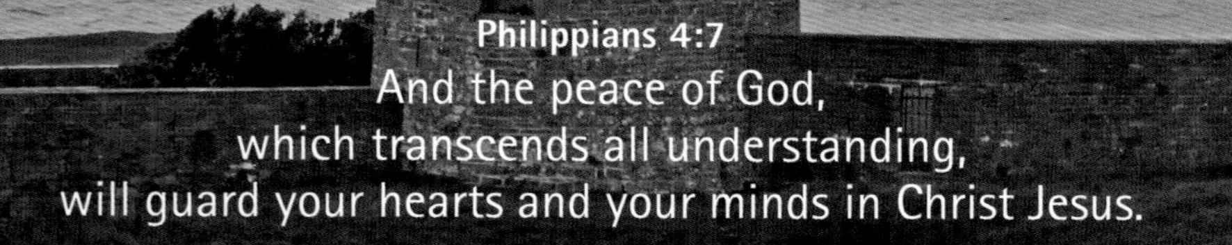
Philippians 4:7
And the peace of God,
which transcends all understanding,
will guard your hearts and your minds in Christ Jesus.
(New International Version)

Bless me, Lord

Psalm 115:15

May the LORD who created the heavens and the earth give you his blessing.

(Contemporary English Version)

Photo: Jonathan Leach, Autumn Leaves

A Prayer of Saint Columba

Be, Lord Jesus,
a bright flame before me,
a guiding star above me,
a smooth path below me,
a kindly shepherd behind me,
today, tonight, and forever.

Saint Columba (521–597)
was a Gaelic Irish missionary monk and one
of the Twelve Apostles of Ireland.
Columba is the patron saint of Derry, Ireland,
where he founded a monastic settlement c. 540.

To:

Numbers 6:24-26

May the Lord bless you and protect you.
May the Lord smile on you and be gracious to you.
May the Lord show you his favour
and give you his peace.

(New Living Translation)

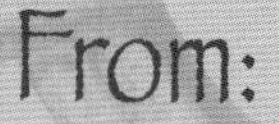